Becoming Spring Again

Cynthia Rodriguez

Instagram @poetry.by.cynthia

Also by Cynthia Rodriguez
The Flowers Will Bloom
Within The Walls

Dearest Reader,

You are not alone. Your pain is heard and felt.

I hope you feel seen in my words—and that you find hope within them.

Self-love is a light that will help guide you out of the dark.

It is time for you to *become spring again.*

Table of contents

Winter
in
Summer

you and I used to be magic
you took me so high I could see heaven,
but it was hell when it happened

you walked away with my heart in hand
and with each step, the sound of my heartbeat
became fainter

when footsteps become an eerie echo, like
ghosts haunting

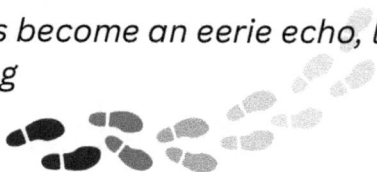

you left on a hot summer day,
and I rooted myself to the ground—waiting
as if you would come back to save me
from the drought

but you never did

I awoke to the sound of your voice
but I found myself alone with the
emptiness of the room
and I realized that it was only in my sleep
that I could see you again

so I chained myself to the bed and stayed
there for days

I never wanted to awaken when I learned
that to dream is to be with you again

if my heart forgets you,
then what will it have to hold
your love is all I've ever known

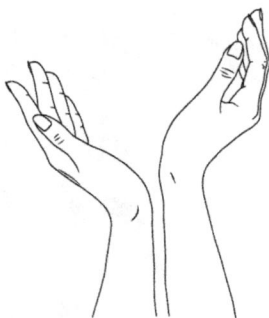

you showed up with a shovel and duct tape
yet I still let you in

*foolish heart of mine—why do you continue
to plunge into the arms of the wrong person?*

my blood drapes every piece of furniture in your home
scratches cover your walls from when my nails screeched at the sound of you breaking my heart

yet I still continued to stay in the house that is not a home

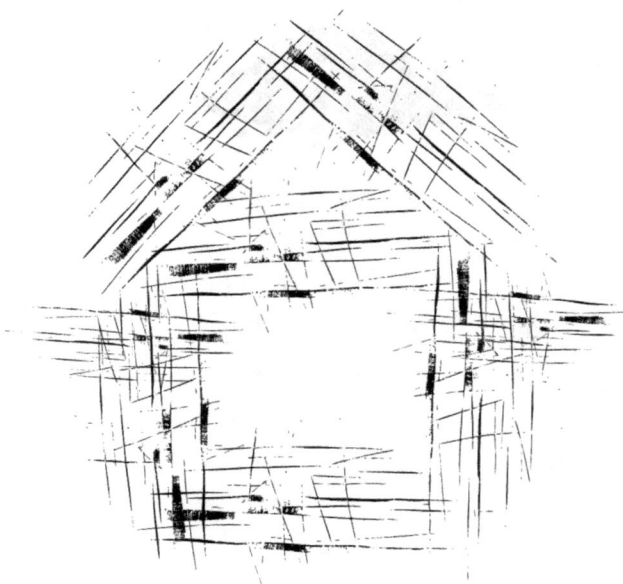

I knocked on your door until you finally answered
can you give them back,
 I begged

my lungs, I need them

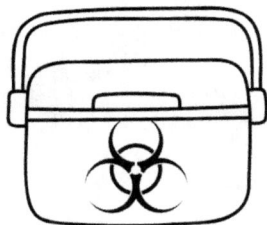

when you left the sun fell from
the sky

you said you were sorry again for ripping
my heart out
and you returned it to me duct taped to keep
it from falling apart
I take it and place it next to all the other hearts
of mine that I had to grow each time you ripped
it out
and I foolishly accept your apology again,
knowing my new heart will have the same fate

our hearts take the worst of the beatings
if only we'd listen when they speak

my heart fell out as I chased after you
and despite its cries, I still chose you

the distance that separates us is cruel
I cannot see you, but I feel your presence—
yet I cannot feel your touch

take it, I begged
take my heart with you if you please
just don't leave it here shattered

because I won't know what to do with
the pieces

my heart sits vacant
its tenant moved out and it refuses to let anyone
else in
the only one it welcomes is the knock of the
ghost of you

I didn't just wear my heart on my sleeve
with you—I dissected it just to show you
all of its contents
but you left it there, open to bleed

I take it back, he said
give me the words I threw at you
I didn't mean it

I can't, I said
I've already devoured them.

I told him I had a sweet tooth, so he laced his
bitter words with sugar
and I consumed them all just for the sweetness
that followed

the wind blows hail at my window,
awakening the memories from the day you left—
the sound of you dropping fragments of my
heart along the way

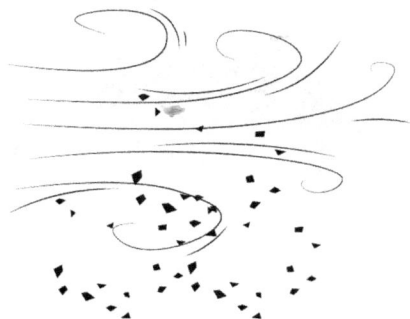

flowerless blooms, entangled roots in the
thought of you

you left me, a stem and thorns
then you went off to pick a different flower,
complaining that you didn't want to get pricked
anymore

seeing you with her felt like a storm cloud
hovering over me—depriving me of the sun,
drowning me in the flood

and no matter how fast I ran, I could never
outrun it

you let me in like the wind on a hot summer day—
refreshing,
but never meant to stay

you stole my heart from me
but you face no charges for the burglary
you remain free, while I remain empty

I even foolishly stayed waiting—
hands reaching
in case you'd return to me

the clouds stole the sun from my eyes again
the breeze stole the season and scared
nature's beauty away
flowers continued to wither, whispering
goodbye as if they would not come back for
their next life

what my life has looked like since the day you left

the curtains close as soon as they see me walk
into the room
the furniture lights a fire knowing a cold draft will
follow

in a fairy tale story, I think I'd be the beast
not because of a curse born of vanity
but because living in the dark for so long
changes you

how do I take, when all I've ever done my entire life is give?

how do I accept when all I've ever done is run?

my heart is not something that I can simply take
out and wash clean
I have to let it bleed through the wounds you left
to get rid of the thoughts of you before I allow
them to close
I do not dare allow them to close while you're still
inside

there you go again silently creeping up on me
just when I thought tonight I would sleep
you make it clear I do not own my tranquility
I plead with you to leave
but my demands are useless—
you're already sinking your claws in deep

vanish, he demanded
and at the snap of his fingers, I did

I escaped the pit of snakes and fell into your arms—
but they held me in slithers

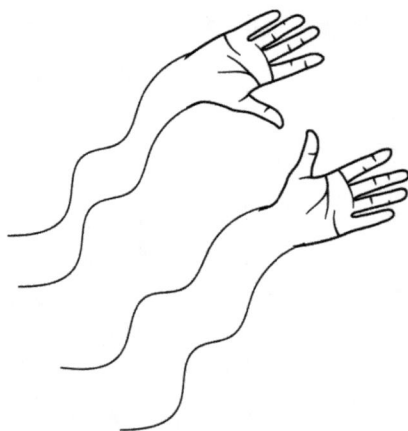

I told you all my stories that were once untold
how I was being haunted by ghosts
you helped me understand that they were my own
invisible demons that just wouldn't go
but I should have known—
when you brought those weapons, promising to
slay them, you'd take my soul in the process

then you'd become the ghost

I buried thoughts of you, but you rose from the dead—
a zombie with an insatiable hunger for my blood

they warned me, I should have had you cremated

when you ghosted me—
I disappeared too

you planted a rose in my heart and promised to
feed it water and love
but that once beautiful rose has now suffered an
immense drought
its shriveled petals have turned to dust and
disappeared in a wind gust
but the thorns stayed embedded deep
causing my heart to plead in agony
demanding to be set free
all at the hands of the man whose promises were
deceit

you left your promises scattered everywhere
and every day I accidentally stumbled across
one and got cut from their jagged edges

broken promises

broken promises—that's what you left me with
I trusted like roses, reaching their hands out to the
first rain shower they'd seen in weeks
but pretty things deceive
you never know if it's trick or treat

it was such a relief to get you out of my system
but when you exited, you went claws out

I bet you're at a fancy restaurant with your new girlfriend
no rooftop, looking at the stars
showing her your painted heart

and I bet you're afraid it will rain, and all your fake will wash away
checking the forecast every hour of the day
I bet you're telling her all these beautiful things
but she doesn't know you're only reciting
you've said all the same to me

you're only performing
and you warmed up right before to hide your cold
rehearsed your words so you get to take her home

and it will only be a matter of time before you send her to the back of the line
leaving her scarred for life
you'll drop the disguise and not even care to hide
but what will you do when all of our flammable tears that you collect with pride catch to your height and begin to ignite

rose petals on the pavement
they're the remnants of yesterday's argument
you raised the vase above your head—
then, crash
our love died at last

it's time for us to let it go
your soft touch turned to thorns
your perfunctory attempts hurt the worst
this is your greatest score
I gave you my entire love, yet you still demand
more

another dinner, table set for two left untouched
except for the broken glass that lies on the rug
and your spilled drink has always been a must
but you don't leave me hungry—you always
make sure I have more than enough
you feed me your words until I'm stuffed,
but mine are hushed
and you want to drag it on like there's no rush
each and every time, it's dwindling trust

I'm the one that has to suppress,
the one who's always left to pick up the mess
and I get cut every time as I gather the words
you threw along, with the broken glass
moistened with wine

and the glass isn't the only thing you leave
shattered
but by morning, you assume none of it mattered
you apologize one more time
you try to justify it—call it a regular couple's
fight
we've cooled off, but after all the gasoline we
threw, we're bound to ignite
you say we're fine, claim our love will defy, recall

the happy times
we go from darkness to sunshine
if we keep burning like this, we'll turn to ash
we may only collide when we crash—
but we crash every time

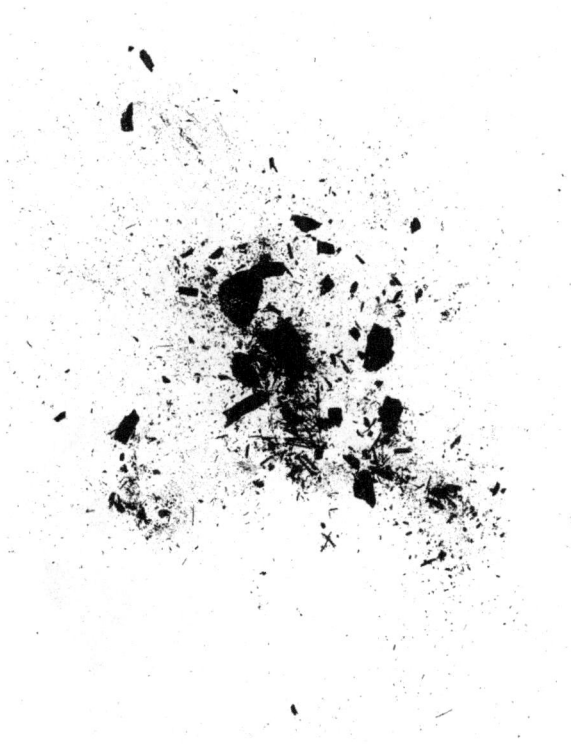

just like tranquility is quiet and peaceful
pain is so loud and disturbing

how can I catch my breath when every day it rains
an umbrella isn't enough to hold this emotional weight

you said I was your flower
I should have known then that you had no
intention of keeping me forever

you always said you didn't like perennials

flowers need the sun too
and you kept me in the dark
to wither away

we were told
that beauty lies in the eye of the beholder
and life taught us
that ugly lies in the soul of the owner

first they were sweet and then they turned bitter
words like candy, making me feel like I'm in some
fantasy
that was your strategy to get me

and like a kid I took the bait
I ate all that you gave, even when I didn't like the
taste

vile-tasting words, yet I consumed them like a
treat
when my lips began to burn, I allowed the hurt
and when I wanted to vomit your words out, you
forced them back down
you hovered over me like a stormy cloud
but I was the one who stayed on the ground
I stayed, even though I knew I would drown

to have left sooner would have been to have
loved me
to have saved my heart from being left empty

but I'm still learning

you left so long ago, but not before you signed
your name on my heart
needle and ink, you embedded yourself deep
now you still lay there, a scar

so many seasons, so many years, so many tears
but none have ever been able to erase that part
some memories you want to stay, some you beg
to fade
but they remain
ghosts haunting and they're the ones you can't
sage
never enough cleansing, my heart is forever
tainted even after turning the page

your presence and your absence brought pain
but I will only remember you as a tragic stain
the shirt that couldn't be saved

trying to save us was water and detergent
down the drain
so many attempts, but it was useless—you
will never again coordinate with
my closet

Beast
within

the storm came rushing in without any warning
roaring winds destroying all, enough rainfall
to force you to swim if you wanted to live
they named her—*anxiety*

my heart went to my mind and said,
here is the key—I'll set you free
but instead, my mind pulled my heart into the cage
and threw away the key
now they sit there, prisoners to my thoughts—

how they became enemies

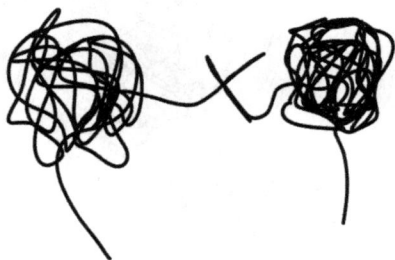

soulless creature, why must you continue to lurk
in the depths of my mind?

why haven't the pints of my blood you've already
consumed quenched your thirst?

why must you demand more?

why do you always demand to be heard?

invisible to my eyes, so loud in my mind

blood—if you don't see it,
 well then she's not hurting

but she's bleeding internally,
silently drowning

sunlight feels cold on my
skin today
last night felt like a nightmare I wouldn't be able
to escape
and now I'm awake, but I still feel this pain

is it possible to drown in air?
because I'm out of the water, but I feel this
tightness in my throat that suffocates
a weight too heavy to bear
I want to expel, but instead I'm forced to swallow
my mistakes

I pick up the mask I've prepared to wear
I do so well making sure no one knows it's fake
because to smile is easier than having to explain

my heart paces around and tells my mind it's too loud, but you wouldn't know, as you can't hear a single sound

but my heart and my mind scream to be free
prisoners to my thoughts, nowhere to flee
curled up, I bite my knees 'til they bleed
and I can't find a way to keep this heartbeat of mine steady
silence, please, I plead

but my heart and my mind become enemies
they refuse to make peace
all at the expense of my tranquility

and I seek remedy, build courage within me,
demand those thoughts to leave
but they dig deeper into me
like thirsty roots, they go searching
but only my blood can quench their thirst
and even then they come back for more
they show no mercy for what they've already left so injured
and when I ask why, they tell me the answer is in

the mirror
so I decide to hate her

my words become monsters
they fill the room, making it darker

and they consume me with such a starvation,
but nothing satisfies their hunger
these thoughts of mine always have an appetite
eating my mind doesn't suffice

they also crave my soul
and when I grip tight, telling them that's mine,
they sharpen their knives, haunt me through the
night, despite my cries
they prepare for the heist
and I have nowhere to hide
because how do you run away from your own
mind?
I've definitely tried, but my mind can be a
stubborn parasite

and people tell me to just turn off the lights
but that's where the monsters reside

not commendable advice

tears escape my eyes
I tried to contain them inside, but they feared
the monsters that are out of sight
they hide in the depths of my mind
invisible, but they're there, lurking

and my eyes burst, tears rolling, overflowing
the pain keeps growing
but I wear the mask,
making sure my hurt
is not showing
I become a recluse so I
don't have to silence
the sound of my emotions exploding
so I can let the tears stream and let my heart
breathe

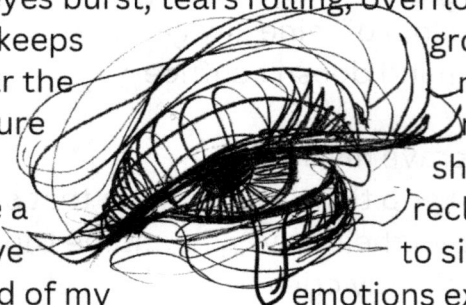

to catch a break, evade the question of whether
I'm okay
then I dry my eyes, keep my heart quiet by tying
it tight, and go back to wearing that disguise

sometimes I feel like I'm a version of Cinderella
not the fairy-tale kind but one that's more
melancholic
during the day I can play dress-up, wear the mask
when life becomes a masquerade
but my demons are never late, and when the
clock strikes twelve they emerge from the depths
of my mind where they hide
all the happy faces I wear fall off a pumpkin
hope flees like a scurrying mouse
and I'm back to facing the judgment that screams
in my ears
but there are no evil stepsisters, it's me alone
with my mind

and as for the glass slipper it remains where I
dropped it,

for no one is looking for me

I fade away into yesterday
the sun has come up, but I'm stuck in the past
some memories you can't erase
and some are gone too fast
time is borrowed, but for life you still have to pay
and the fees are vast
wounds can heal, but the scars stay
reminders of the impact of every crash
and I'm sailing into the ocean's never-ending waves
no anchor can keep me steadfast

because I'm a ghost that disappeared so long ago

I watch as raindrops on my window roll
down they go,
some breaking apart with the wind, proving fragile
while others stay still and not agile
I watch, fingers pressed against my window,
wondering if they're frozen in melancholy or grace
I trace them with my fingertips as if trying to
capture them in an embrace
I look at the skies and ask them to translate
I cannot understand this rain

I ask the raindrops on my window to speak to me
to tell me a story
help ease my worries

I watch as the glass begins to fog, and my hands
freeze
it's cold out, it seems
well I wouldn't have known, because I'm stuck
here looking through my window, my reflection
looking right back
and I still can't understand that the skies are clear,
the sun shines bright, but my eyes aren't dry
I can't see that the raindrops on my window are
me

To tame the beasts that lurk within me would be to finally breathe, instead of just expelling all the air my lungs beg me to keep.

in this maze I try to find my way
battling thoughts entangled with my demons
and I follow the signs that say, escape
but even then, it's not that easy
like a toddler learning to walk, I will still fall
I may be okay today, but tomorrow I may have
to crawl
running away from your own mind is the hardest
of all

life has a price, and what I'm not charged today,
tomorrow I'll be charged twice
forever in debt, always having to pay interest
but I still get to choose how my life will be lived
and I choose to fight it, not let my strength be
diminished
but there will always be times when I stumble,
as I am still human

and it's okay to have to be reminded

Bullets

bones surround me
the remains of all the positive thoughts I
murdered
I dismembered them like a beast that welcomes
only the darkness

if I gave all my petals to you, then what would the next person receive?

and so I know I'm damaged goods
I label myself with an expiration date, so no one will want me

I feel hands reaching, tossing me around like
produce, for no one wants the bruised ones
*take all the pretty ones first, leave her for last
the resort*

don't eat that—that's too much
eat this—that's not enough
change your clothes again, the ones you've
chosen aren't flattering
if only you were thinner, if only you were curvier
if only you looked more like her

who let you out—go hide from everyone's sight

words we speak to the mirror

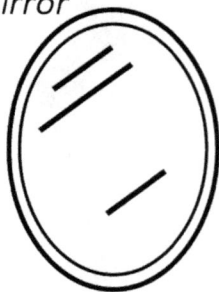

I see compliments wrapped in vines of thorns
and negative thoughts wrapped with pretty
little bows

chained at the leg, the mirror gave me a choice—
a key if I gave it one compliment, or a chainsaw

I picked up the chainsaw, determined to cut
through the bone

I circled the parts of me I didn't like

the little girl who saw me thought I had a really cool Halloween costume

why won't you heal, I asked my wounds
because you keep bringing us back to
the source, they replied

I kept your shirt and wore it to sleep, no wonder I was always cold

my body knew before my mind did

and yet I still let it shiver

I tried to swallow some self-love today, but I
ended up choking on it
I had to spit it back out

but the negative thoughts — those went down
smoothly

I see all the signs that a storm is coming
darkening of the skies, cloud movement, angry
winds, thunder in the distance
plenty of time to evade, yet I stay

my heart tells me the forecast,
but I don't listen

where are the kind hearts—I cannot find them
you're looking in the wrong place,
whispered my heart

yet I placed it where I knew it would hurt

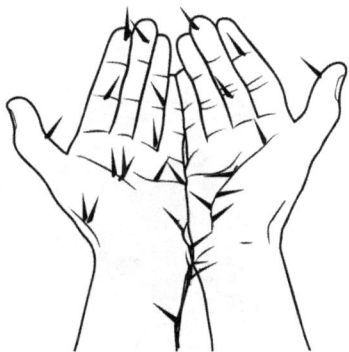

I was stuffed from all of your words
so I saved the ones you continued to throw in a
jar and put them in the freezer

every now and then I take them out and eat
them because I only know how to feel whole
when I'm shattered

and here I am loading the gun that is
aimed at me

*bullets—the words we speak to
ourselves*

It's not you,
it's me

it's not you, it's me—the excuse that's used
when you simply aren't interested

except for—

it really was me

though your hands were gentle,
my heart was fragile

had I given it to you back then,
it would have crumbled with your touch—
and you didn't deserve to hold emptiness

I wanted to tell you I missed you that day
my heart even jumped from my chest, in search
of your arms
but I caged it back in, proclaiming it wasn't
allowed to feel that way

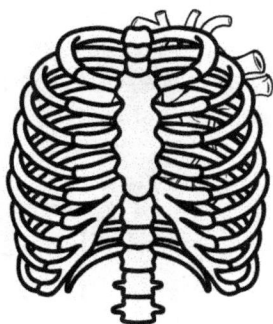

when the sun sets—the walls cave in
you emerge from under my bed
your absence lies right beside me
the bed sheets become sandpaper rubbing
against my skin, depriving me of sleep
the banging at the door is all the love you gave
me that I refused to let in

the memories of regrets that still haunt me

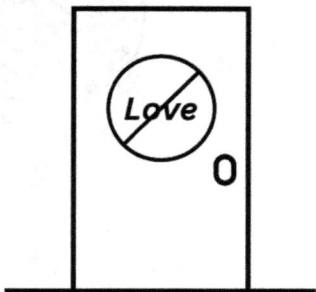

to feel undeserving of love is a punishment you
inflict upon yourself

someone will love the parts of you others didn't

someone will hold your heart when it trembles

someone will find beauty in the bruised fruit

someone will choose you

A heart that bloomed

hollow was the sound of my heart when he came
knocking
summer was the season, winter was the feeling
but love was all he gave, while others would take
and take

true love's kiss awoke me from being frozen in
another time

you came with needle and thread and said you'd
stitch me back up every time I fell apart

your hands and fingertips dance with mine
we talk under the stars, captivated by the
moonlight
we watch the night send the moon away for
sunrise
and I'm right where I want to be
I swear I can feel both of our hearts beating in
sync
when I'm with you I'm in serenity
you are my serendipity
when my mind is a beast you're my tranquility
you're the one who puts my worry at ease
the one that makes me believe in me

just hearing your name makes my heart grow feet
and run off to find you

I told you about the darkness in my life
but you didn't run
instead you stole the sun from the sky and gave
it to me

you held my heart with your bare hands, even
though it was in flames
you didn't care if you got burned
you only focused on removing the hurt

you are more than just a thought
you are a presence that has made a home of me
and I placed a welcome mat for you, because my
heart has never been this inviting to another soul
before
its curtains have always stayed closed
but for you my heart flutters in the best way
it cannot be tamed
it demands to let the light in
to see the sky from the deck with you
and when my heart is tired it knows it has
another home in your arms

the image of you appears in my mind throughout
the day
butterflies play the piano in my stomach
and thoughts of you bring my smile to life

whispers from the sky
we're caught in the twilight
I'm captured in your gaze
we dance as if the moon was never meant to
say goodbye
we long for a never-ending night
first it's nature, then you and I
the rest of the world isn't synchronized
it's like we're living in a different time

I've traveled oceans to get to you
all the heartbreak that brought me tears had me
swimming for my life
I fought the beastly waves in my brain
anchored my heart to the deepest part of the sea
so I wouldn't drift away
I swam relentlessly and never gave in to the
vicious winds

but at last I'm in your arms, where heartbreak is
unknown
I fought for what might await me at the end of the
storm
but it was you who pulled me out of it so I
wouldn't have to fight anymore
you threw your arms like a float so that I could
grab hold
and I only knew of the cold in the freezing storm,
but now your arms keep me warm

my heart is now free, no longer a prisoner of the
sea
bleeding wounds have begun healing
from roaring winds my life became serene
and it is all because of you
your kind heart, nurturing soul, and unfailing
presence make me complete _____ ❤ ˅ _____

you came, weapons in hand, ready to slay my
demons
you didn't even put a suit of armor on, you were
ready to fight no matter the damage that would
come to you

your kindness is like a ray of sunlight
peeking into the darkest night

your name is written gently on my heart
your heart has made my soul its home

the light bulb was flickering
I squeezed your hand and you pulled me close
we're going in, you said
I'll stay with you even if the light burns out
and we dove right into the darkest depths of my
mind
to free all the thoughts of him, them, everyone,
and everything that was harming me
and it only got darker before we found the
tiniest speck of light

but as you promised—you never left

the moon is a beauty tonight
but you don't take your eyes off me

and I realize how I found love in the dark

my heart flaps its wings at the thought of you
I feel like a butterfly emerging from its cocoon

you have awoken feelings I didn't even know were
sleeping

your words tasted like cotton candy
and I waited for a bitter aftertaste, but it
never came
I didn't know you could indulge in sweet,
kind words without enduring the taste of the
sour ones

*the realization that you were settling for
less*

the arms of your words hold me close
you are the only one to have seen my soul
others have received my heart but never
me in whole

the sea gazes at the moon and speaks,

I wish I could see you all day
capture you in my waves
allow you to sink into my embrace
but the sun is jealous, and she breaks our gaze

and I lose sight of you until the following day
but the skies also forbid our love, and they hide
you from me in the clouds
your tears—the rain
and in every splash I feel your heart's ache
I hear your soul scream

allow me to set you free
forget about the rest of the world and only create
my tides
you're the only light that I need to thrive

may you be loved like the sea loves the moon

and you said to me,
I am the sea and you are my moon

If I were a mermaid with the desire
to have feet, would you save me
from the sea

I first knew I loved you when we sat in the twilight
gazing at the sky, your eyes like magnets pulled mine
and my heart was screaming happiness in sync with my mind for the very first time
two souls intertwined
with a kiss I knew you were mine
my thoughts aligned
no confusion in my mind
just you and me, collecting moments
time could freeze, and it would be an art piece
with the sight of you before me

you took this stray heart of mine in when you
found it shivering out in the cold
I fall asleep in your arms because they feel like
home
intertwined with your love, I'll never let this
soul of mine roam

Become Spring

my pessimistic thoughts lead me astray
but whispers from the garden call my name
birds follow, collecting traces of me as I enter
the gates
they carry my broken pieces as if holding a
bride's wedding dress train
I can hear them strain as they carry my weight

I feel lighter with every step, wondering if I'll
make it
a breeze suddenly crashes into me, causing my
body to weaken
as I stumble, the grass intertwines, leaving
 its roots—they raise me high
they lead me to the sunflowers, who whisper,
 never give up

the grass unravels as I'm placed back on my feet
the lilies point to the peonies that
stand, gathering pieces of me

all the flowers begin to circle in

I feel the butterflies dust pollen on me as if I'm
to bloom
the whispers continue, and I very vividly hear,

the pollen is you

the butterflies, finding beauty in my broken, fed
off it like nectar
collecting pollen in the process, storing it to
later be brushed onto me

every living thing in the garden lifts its roots,
showing me the pieces I threw out were used as
compost

all of my being lies in the garden, thriving
and in synchrony they all say,

the pollen is you, and you are also the bloom

I want to be my own blanket when I'm cold
my own wrecker when I'm stranded or stuck
the map when I'm lost
the tenant and home

but asking for help when you need
it is also a strength

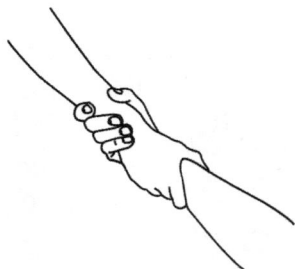

he asks,
does he make you feel the way I do?
to which she responds,
no, because then I'd feel an immense pain
embedded so deep in me that it could never be
excised
you'd have to rip me apart to get to the roots that
have dug into my flesh and entangled every
nerve running through my body

you deserve better

they cause pain when they stay
it causes pain to excise them

but choosing to remove them
is choosing yourself

thorns—
the people who only bring harm to your life

your heart is a gift to those who deserve it
so know the value of it and don't give it to
people who will simply throw it into the pile of
gifts they deem unnecessary

you were not there when I needed you
and when I shut the door, you wouldn't stop
knocking
but even if I open the door now, it will always
be too late
you will only be met by a cold draft, for I am
long gone

true love's kiss revives, it doesn't sentence
you to a curse or offer you a poisonous apple

so don't settle for belittlement or deception

charming can be deceiving
but don't worry—there are men with integrity
you just have to wait patiently
don't rush things be wise
open your eyes—don't let pretty things blind

for some time, your heart will carry an ache
trust will be a struggle to regain
but one day, a smile will come and never fade—
from the one who's meant to stay

those who love you will not only walk through
the light with you, but through the dark
and they will hold your hand while doing so

don't settle for someone who only wants the
bright pieces of you and not the dark

in that case, you might as well always be
shattered, as they will never take you in whole

couples fight all the time
they say things they don't mean,
and lose sleep over it at night

but you can't choose and then unchoose who you
love
it's not just a change of mind—
your heart's in control the whole time

so if you say you don't want me,
you're confused, unsure what to do...
well, then it's not meant to be

because I want someone who wants me
wholeheartedly—
not just a piece of me

you do not have to separate your fragile pieces
from your strong ones

together, they are what make you whole

in a sky full of stars,
see me as the moon

lungs were meant to have their breath
taken away only temporarily so it could
dance in the sky, gather light, and come
back to give you life
not stolen by those who will crush them
beneath their feet until your worth's
deprived

the blaze came strong, destroying everything
in its path
made ashes of my dreams
I felt the scorching pain as it consumed the
hope from within me
the courage that took years to build was ash
within minutes
I pleaded with life, *why*

*why is building so much more difficult than
destroying?*
*why must progress take years to build, yet
vanish in minutes?*

scorched and defeated I take a look at the
embers that remain
it is then that I realize I am those embers
engulfed by my own flames
in fear of my own strength, I let myself
incinerate
let my mind stray at an endless pace
but I will not let those thoughts have the final
say

this fire in me will not die
though I may get burned from time to time,

the embers are still there so they can always revive

don't let anyone keep the sun from you and deprive your roots of the love they deserve

you deserve better than to be someone's wilted flower

wilted flowers upon the dry soil appear ready
to shrivel to nothing
but their roots are still there, fighting
but you only see the weak

*being fragile is being strong, for it takes great
strength not to wither away*

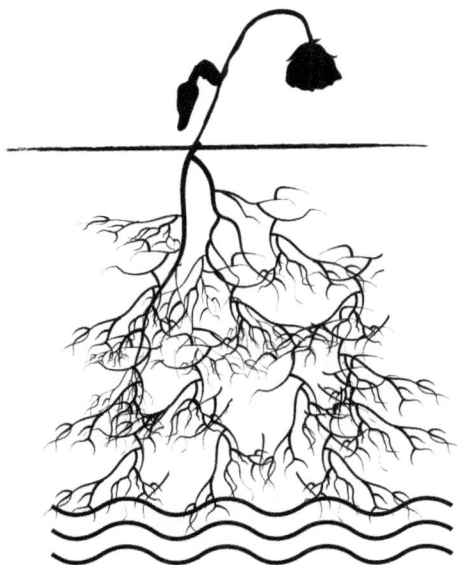

your scars are warriors that helped you
conquer many battles
the proof is in the writing inscribed on your
body, heart, and soul

I'll never let this heart of mine be anything less
cruel words can go hunting, but I won't let
them catch me

you'll find me in meadows, a wildflower
blooming and thriving without human
intervention
just the love of her own

wilts in nature's environment

but she always comes back

I've built houses out of the words people have thrown at me
and I used so much of my strength building them
but now they sit there, vacant

you do not have to stay in the places that cause you pain just because you've put so much into them

learning to accept compliments helps heal
your heart
but don't use them to replace the words you
speak to yourself
no one should speak kinder to you than
yourself

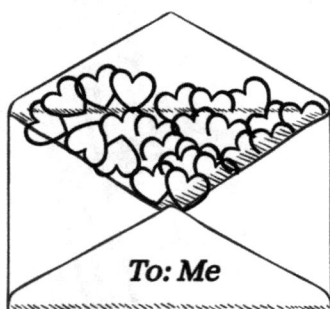

I'll plant, feed, and protect seeds in my heart because how can anyone love me if I'm empty

She grew blooms from her wounds.

it's much easier to allow yourself to be consumed by the pain.

so you will not come out of this ruined; you will come out a warrior

strength is like a seed—
delicate at first, but as it sprouts and grows, it
becomes more resilient

she traveled far
but far within herself
a journey of discovery
a smile so unfamiliar
a smile that was her own
the joy that filled her soul was one that she
had never known
when they broke her, they took everything,
leaving only a heart that was torn

self-discovery

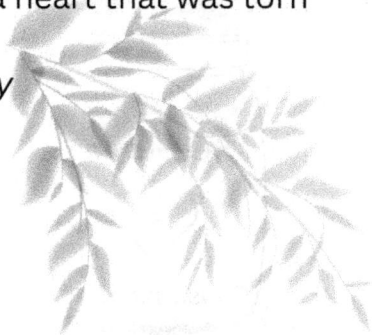

I'll fill my heart with self-love,
and watch as it blooms

Self-love

Consume daily

stop waiting for life to get easy
there is nothing easy about what you do and
conquer every day
difficult does not lessen the value of
something

if I could be invisible, I'd choose to be the wind
no matter where you go, you'd always feel me,
even in my absence

to fear is to live, because fear awakens the
silence in you
when your heart goes dormant, it is awoken
by the tremors that knock on its door
and letting them in isn't always the best, but
it is a reminder that you are alive
and sometimes we are afraid of losing what
we love most
and we should welcome that fear, because to
love deeply is to fear losing it

open your arms to the kind words that come
your way
it can be hard when your mind is caged with the
thoughts that won't let go
but feed your heart and mind enough love—

flowers will bloom, overcoming the weeds

the last petals of the season fall

and I smile knowing that come spring,
everything will bloom again

winter doesn't just leave,
it becomes spring

Dear reader,

Thank you for reading my book. I hope you enjoyed it!

If you have a moment, I'd really appreciate it if you could leave your honest review and/or rating on Amazon.
Reviews help other readers decide whether my book is right for them, while also supporting me as an indie author.

I'd love to hear your thoughts.

With gratitude,

Cynthia

www.ingramcontent.com/pod-product-compliance
Lightning Source LLC
Chambersburg PA
CBHW060321050426
42449CB00011B/2583